JEALOUS

First published 1990
by Cherrytree Press Ltd
Windsor Bridge Road
Bath, Avon BA2 3AX England

Copyright © Cherrytree Press Ltd 1990

First published in the United States 1991
by Raintree Publishers

Copyright © 1991 Raintree Publishers Limited Partnership

Library of Congress Number: 90-46540

1 2 3 4 5 6 7 8 9   95 94 93 92 91

Library of Congress Cataloging-in-Publication Data

Amos, Janine.
   Feelings/by Janine Amos; illustrated by Gwen Green.
   Cover title.
   Contents: [1] Afraid—[2] Angry—[3] Hurt—[4] Jealous—[5] Lonely—[6] Sad.
   1. Emotions—Case studies—Juvenile literature. [1. Emotions.]
I. Green, Gwen, ill.   II. Title.
BF561.A515   1991
152.4—dc20   90-46540
                                                  CIP
                                                  AC

   ISBN 0-8172-3775-5 (v. 1); ISBN 0-8172-3776-3 (v. 2); ISBN 0-8172-3777-1 (v. 3); ISBN 0-8172-3778-X (v. 4); ISBN 0-8172-3779-8 (v. 5); ISBN 0-8172-3780-1 (v. 6).

JEALOUS

By Janine Amos
Illustrated by Gwen Green

RAINTREE PUBLISHERS
Milwaukee

KELLY'S STORY

"Hurry up!" called Kelly's dad. "You'll be late!"

Kelly's dad always took her and her sister to school. But today it was just Kelly. Sarah had chicken pox.

"What will Sarah do all day?" asked Kelly.

"She'll stay in bed and sleep a lot," said Kelly's dad.

Kelly climbed into the car.

"Will Mommy stay with her?" she asked.

"Yes," said Kelly's dad, "Mom will take care of her."

"I suppose Mommy will read her stories," said Kelly. "I suppose they'll eat toast and drink hot chocolate together."

Kelly's dad smiled. But Kelly didn't think it was funny.

When Kelly got home from school, she ran up to Sarah's bedroom. Sarah was asleep. She looked very warm and cozy. On the bed there were two big storybooks and a new comic book.

"I wish I had chicken pox," thought Kelly.

Why does Kelly wish she had chicken pox?

After supper, Aunt Mary came to visit. She had brought Sarah a funny get-well card and some grapes. Kelly liked grapes.

"I don't feel well, either!" said Kelly. But everyone laughed.

Kelly took the grapes upstairs. Sarah was still asleep. Her face was red and spotty. Kelly sat at the end of Sarah's bed. She looked at the grapes. They were big fat green ones, with no seeds. Slowly Kelly slipped a grape into her mouth. Then another and another. Soon there were only two grapes left.

Was Kelly hungry? Why do you think she ate the grapes?

Kelly went into her own room. She felt grouchy. She was mad at herself for eating the grapes, and she was mad at Sarah for being sick.

Just then, Kelly's dad came in. He sat down next to Kelly. But he didn't smile.

"You aren't very nice to your little sister, are you?" her dad said. "Last week you ruined her drawing. Yesterday you broke her doll. And today you ate her grapes." Kelly turned red.

"Why do you do it, Kelly?" asked her dad.

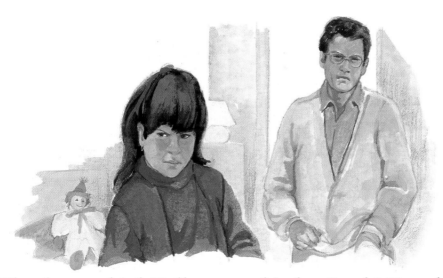

Why do you think Kelly was unkind to Sarah? How does Kelly feel now?

Kelly's dad waited. It was very quiet. Kelly knew it was important to talk.

"Sarah always gets everything," Kelly said at last. "You and Mommy are always talking about her. You don't care about me!"

Kelly's dad put his arm around her.

"I'm sorry you feel like that," he said. "But you're wrong. Mom and I love both of you. We have to do more things for Sarah because she's only five. But we love you just as much." Her dad smiled. "Wait here!" he said.

Her dad came back with a big box. Inside there were lots of photographs. He pointed to one of them.

"Remember this? That's you," he said to Kelly, "when you had chicken pox. You were only two years old."

"That was before Sarah was even born!" Kelly said.

"Yes," her dad answered. "You were very special to us then, and you still are."

Together they looked at the photograph.

"I had lots of spots," said Kelly, laughing.

Why do you think Kelly's father showed her the pictures?

Kelly looked at all the pictures in the box. Some were of her mom and dad. Some were of Aunt Mary and Grandma. But most of them were of Kelly when she was little.

"Did you take all these pictures of me?" asked Kelly.

"Yes, most of them," her dad said. "Tomorrow let's buy a photograph album and put them in it."

"Great!" said Kelly.

Before bedtime, Kelly gave her dad a big hug.
"Can we take some pictures tomorrow?" she asked.
"Sure," said her dad. "What shall we photograph?"
"Sarah, of course! With chicken pox!" Kelly laughed.

How do you think Kelly feels now?

Feeling like Kelly

Have you ever felt the way Kelly did? It's called feeling jealous. Jealousy is a powerful feeling. It can make you sad, angry, and lonely all at once. It never makes you happy.

Jealousy grows

Jealousy can grow. It grows in your imagination. Kelly was jealous of Sarah. She imagined Sarah was having a good time—even when Sarah was sick.

Jealousy spoils things

Jealousy can spoil things. It can spoil friendships. If you think someone has something you don't have, you may want to hurt them. Kelly thought her parents loved Sarah best. That's why she was mean to her sister. But being mean didn't help Kelly. It only made her unhappy with herself.

Think about it

Read the stories in this book. Think about the people in them. Do you sometimes feel the way they do? Next time you feel jealous, ask yourself some questions: What am I jealous of? Am I really missing out on anything? Who can I talk to so I can feel better?

DANNY'S STORY

It was Christmas morning! Danny opened his eyes and jumped out of bed.

"Wake up, Luke!" he shouted to his cousin. "I'll race you downstairs!"

Luke was two years older than Danny. But he was just as excited about Christmas. The two boys pulled on their clothes and ran down the hall.

"Less noise, you two!" called a grown-up.

But Danny and Luke didn't hear. They were already halfway down the stairs, heading for the big Christmas tree. All their presents were under that tree, just waiting to be opened.

Soon the floor was covered with wrapping paper and toys. Then Luke jumped up. He ran to the other end of the room. There, side by side, were two huge presents.

"Quick, Danny!" he shouted. "There's one for each of us."

Opening this one was hard work. But soon Danny had done it, and in front of him stood a brand new red bike. Tied to the handlebars was a message: MERRY CHRISTMAS, DANNY, FROM MOM AND DAD.

"Just what I wanted!" said Danny.

How do you think Danny feels?

Danny turned to watch Luke. His cousin was just pulling his bike out of the wrappings. Danny opened his eyes wide. It was the most beautiful bike he'd ever seen! It was blue with white wheels and a red seat. And on the side was painted "Road Rocket."

"Wow! That's much better than mine!" Danny thought.

Soon everyone else was awake. They all came down to see the boys' presents.

"Aren't you two lucky?" said Luke's dad.

"I'm going out right after breakfast," Luke said. "I can't wait to ride my Road Rocket."

"I'll come out later," said Danny.

How is Danny feeling now? Have you ever felt like this?

Danny watched Luke wheel the Road Rocket out the door. Then he looked at his pile of presents and his own new red bike. Danny had everything he'd asked for. He knew he should be happy. But instead he felt mad.

"Why does Luke get everything really special?" he thought. "It's not fair."

All day Danny stayed inside. He did a jigsaw puzzle. He watched TV. He played a game with his uncle. And all the time he thought about Luke's blue and white Road Rocket. The more he thought about it, the more he wanted to ride it.

Just before bedtime, Danny crept out into the dark hall. He put his hand on the Road Rocket's shiny frame.

"Danny!" said a voice.

Danny jumped. It was his mother.

"I was only looking, Mom," he said quickly. "There's nothing wrong with that, is there?" He felt a little guilty.

What do you think Danny's mother will say?

"So you wish you had Luke's bike, do you?" asked Danny's mother. Danny didn't know what to say.

"Don't worry," she said. "Everyone feels like that sometimes—grown-ups too. It's natural."

"It's not a very good feeling," said Danny.

"I know," said his mother. "You just have to try to enjoy what you have. Go for a ride with Luke tomorrow. I'll bet your bike works just as well as a Road Rocket."

It was true. Danny looked at his red bike and smiled.

"It's got a name too," he said.

"Oh?" asked his mother. "What is it?"

"I'll call it the Fire Jet!" said Danny.

Feeling like Danny

Have you ever wanted something that belonged to someone else? Have you ever thought that something your sister, brother, or friend had was nicer than anything you owned? Most people have felt that way sometimes—adults too. It's often hard to know what to do about it. You start to think, "It's not fair!"

What can you do?

When you're feeling like this, it helps to think of all the ways in which you *are* lucky. You could make a list of all the things you have that make you feel good. Or you could try talking about your feelings with someone you trust, just as Danny did.

KATE'S STORY

Kate and Jenny were walking to school. Their schoolbags were heavy, and it was very warm. But Kate and Jenny didn't notice. They were planning what to do at lunchtime.

"After you eat, you could come to my house," said Kate.

"Let's go to the park," said Jenny.

"And do what?" Kate asked.

"Play marbles!" they both shouted together.

Kate and Jenny were best friends. Their parents were friends too. The two girls went to the same school. They liked the same things, and their favorite game was marbles.

After eating lunch, Kate met Jenny in front of her house.

"Let's go!" said Kate. She was excited.

"Wait a minute," said Jenny.

"What for?" asked Kate.

"Kim's coming with us," said Jenny. "I asked her."

That bothered Kate.

"Why? We don't need her," she said.

"I like her," said Jenny.

"Well, I don't," said Kate. "We can't play marbles now."

"Sure, we can," Jenny said. "Three can play."

Why is Kate feeling bothered?

Soon Kim arrived. She was out of breath from running.
"Sorry I'm late!" said Kim.

Jenny smiled. She took Kim's hand in hers. But Kate didn't smile. She stuck her hands in her pockets and turned away.

On the way to the park, Kate was very quiet. She walked behind the other two girls and watched them.

"Jenny likes Kim more than me," she thought. She kicked a stone with her foot.

How does Kate feel? If you were Kate, what would you do now?

Jenny told Kim how they played marbles.

"You can go first," she said. "You can use my aggies."

Kate wished she could hit Kim.

"I hate Kim," she thought. "Jenny never let *me* play with her aggies."

Kate felt sad. When the three of them walked back to school, Kate didn't say much. She went back to class without even saying goodbye.

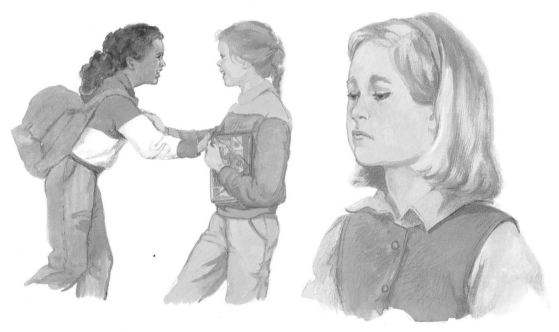

Why doesn't Kate talk to Jenny and Kim?

At recess, Kate felt worse. She wanted to cry. Kate's teacher, Mr. Rose, asked her what was wrong.

"Kim took Jenny away from me," said Kate sadly. And she told him about Jenny and Kim. "I'm all alone."

"You don't have to be," Mr. Rose said. "You can play with both of them. We have to share our friends, Kate, just as we share other things."

Kate thought for a while.

"Why don't we just go and say hi?" asked Mr. Rose.

So Kate and Mr. Rose walked over to where Jenny and Kim were playing.

When Kate and Mr. Rose arrived, Jenny and Kim smiled.

"Can I play with you?" asked Kate, quietly.

"Sure!" said Kim. She took Kate's hand, and Jenny held onto Kate's other hand.

"What are you going to play?" asked Mr. Rose.

"MARBLES!" shouted the three girls.

How did Mr. Rose help Kate?

Feeling like Kate

Have you ever felt like Kate? Sometimes it's hard to share your friends. You want to keep them to yourself. But people aren't like toys. You can't own them.

Making friends

When Jenny asked Kim to play, Kate felt upset. She also was a bit scared. She was scared that Jenny didn't like her anymore. If someone makes a new friend, it doesn't mean they like you less. It's just that they like someone else too!

Talking about it

Jealousy can make you sad and lonely. If you're feeling like this, tell someone. Talk to someone you trust. Kate's teacher knew just how she felt. Someone will understand how you feel too.

Feeling jealous

Think about the stories in this book. Kelly, Danny, and Kate all felt jealous. Talking about it helped them. It could help you.

If you are feeling frightened or unhappy, don't keep it to yourself. Talk to an adult you can trust:

- one of your parents or other relatives
- a friend's parent or other relative
- a teacher
- the principal
- someone else at school
- a neighbor
- someone at a church, temple, or synagogue

You can also find someone to talk to about a problem by calling places called "hotlines." One hotline is **Child Help,** which you can call from anywhere in the United States. Just call

1-800-422-4453

from any telephone. You don't need money to call.

Or look in the phone book to find another phone number of people who can help. Try

- Children and Family Service
- Family Service

Remember you can always call the Operator in any emergency. Just dial 0 or press the button that says 0 on the telephone.